Contents

Introduction   7

  Welcome to the Centennial Year   7

  The 2026 Centennial: Why This Year Is Unmissable   8

Chapter 1: The Essence of Route 66   14

  History and Cultural Significance   14

  Key Facts and Timeline   16

  Essential Traveler Information (Weather, Safety, Permits, Costs)   18

Chapter 2: Planning Your 2026 Centennial Trip   22

  Sample Itineraries (7-Day, 10-Day, 14-Day)   22

  Budgeting and Cost Estimates   28

  Packing Essentials and Preparation Tips   31

  Navigation Tools and Apps   32

Chapter 3: Illinois – Chicago to the Mississippi River   34

  Starting in Chicago: Iconic Kickoff Points   34

  Key Stops and Attractions   36

  Dining, Lodging, and Vehicle-Friendly Options   41

Chapter 4: Missouri – Gateway Arch to Kansas Border   44

  St. Louis and Ozarks Highlights   44

  Must-See Stops and Hidden Gems   47

  Classic Diners, Motels, and Camping Spots   52

Chapter 5: Kansas, Oklahoma, and Texas Panhandle   **56**

    Short Kansas Stretch and Oklahoma Heartland   56

    Amarillo to Texas Icons (Cadillac Ranch, etc.)   59

    Regional Dining, Lodging, and Route Variations   60

Chapter 6: New Mexico and Arizona – Desert Wonders   **62**

    Albuquerque to Petrified Forest   62

    Flagstaff, Grand Canyon Detours, and Oatman   66

    RV/Campervan Boondocking and Motel Recommendations70

Chapter 7: California – Barstow to Santa Monica Pier   **72**

    Mojave Desert to the Pacific   72

    Final Must-See Stops and Celebrations   76

    Endpoint Rituals and Post-Trip Extensions   78

Appendices and Bonus Resources   **84**

    Centennial 2026 Events Calendar   84

    Quick-Reference Charts   85

    Troubleshooting and FAQs   87

    Useful Contacts and Websites   88

Introduction

Welcome to the Centennial Year

The moment I stood at the corner of East Adams Street in Chicago, the official starting point of Route 66, a mix of anticipation and uncertainty hit me like the first engine roar of a long road ahead. It was 2019, and I had a worn paper map, a half-charged phone, and absolutely no idea what I was getting myself into.

Route 66 isn't just a road—it's a living museum, a 2,448-mile story stretching from the skyscrapers of Chicago to the Pacific waves of Santa Monica. When Cyrus Avery and his fellow highway boosters first proposed this diagonal route in 1926, they couldn't have imagined it would become the most famous road in America, perhaps the world. But here we are, one hundred years later, and the mystique has only grown stronger. There's something profoundly moving about following the same path that Dust Bowl families took westward in the 1930s, that postwar vacationers cruised in their gleaming Chevrolets in the 1950s, and that counterculture wanderers explored in painted VW buses in the 1960s. You're not just driving—you're connecting with a century of American dreams, struggles, and endless optimism.

The 2026 Centennial: Why This Year Is Unmissable

The 2026 centennial has transformed Route 66 into a year-long celebration with official events, restorations, and renewed energy across  all eight states. The festivities kicked off dramatically on January 3, 2026, with **The Drive Home VII: Route 66 – A Century of Adventure**, a commemorative caravan of nine vintage vehicles starting in Santa Monica, California, and traveling the full route eastward to Chicago by January 12, 2026, before heading to the Detroit Auto Show for display. This event, organized by America's Automotive Trust, the Detroit Auto Show, and the National Route 66 Centennial Commission, set the tone for the year with cross-country rallies blending history and adventure.

Key national highlights include:

- **April 30 – May 2, 2026**: The National Route 66 Centennial Kickoff in Springfield, Missouri (the "Birthplace of Route 66"), featuring a global livestreamed concert, satellite connections to cities like Joliet (IL), St. Louis (MO), Amarillo (TX), Albuquerque (NM), and Santa Monica (CA), plus family-friendly activities.
- **April 30, 2026**: A major convergence at the Santa Monica Pier around 5 p.m., with commemorative activities, broadcasts, and gatherings for travelers following self-guided or organized routes.
- **June 2026**: The Main Street of America Route 66 Centennial Caravan (from Santa Monica to Chicago) and the Route 66 Centennial Great Race (Chicago to Santa Monica), with participation open to enthusiasts.
- **November 11, 2026**: Official birthday celebrations, including the Illinois Route 66 Scenic Byway Statewide Conference and Centennial in Springfield, IL, plus statewide events honoring the highway's designation.

State-specific efforts abound: Illinois features educational events and a custom centennial logo; Missouri hosts major kickoffs; Oklahoma plans signature festivals like expansions of the AAA Route 66 RoadFest; and California emphasizes beachside concerts, car shows, and closing ceremonies. The Route 66 Preservation Trust and state associations have used funding for restored neon signs, reopened vintage stations, new museums, and monuments like 3D Route 66 shield sculptures. Expect larger crowds, special limited-edition merchandise, pop-up exhibits, and augmented reality experiences—making 2026 the ultimate time to go.

But Let's Be Real: Planning Can Still Be Overwhelming

I've received hundreds of questions from fellow travelers, and I've made plenty of mistakes myself. On my first trip, I rolled out of Chicago in a compact sedan, only to hit unpaved, rutted gravel sections (like optional dirt stretches in New Mexico's Glenrio to San Jon area or Arizona's pre-1950s alignments) that my low-clearance car couldn't handle—I crawled at 10 mph for an hour, fearing suspension damage. Navigation was a nightmare: GPS apps pushed me onto I-40, while Route 66-specific tools contradicted each other on alignments. Lodging? I arrived in Williams, Arizona, on a busy summer Saturday without reservations and paid $289 for a chain hotel when historic motor courts were half the price if booked early.

This guide solves these exact problems. It answers real questions like: Which Oklahoma alignment to choose among three historic routes? Can you drive in an RV without getting stuck? Where are cell dead zones, and what to download offline? Which diners are authentically old-school vs. tourist traps? How to balance icons with hidden local gems?

Tailored for Every Traveler and Vehicle

Whether solo on a Harley, with kids in the backseat, in a vintage convertible, or piloting a 32-foot motorhome, this guide has specifics for you. Route 66 is a patchwork—modern highways, gravel paths, one-lane roads—so vehicle choice matters hugely. Some photogenic sections (e.g., Arizona's unpaved 18-mile pre-1950s stretch west of Seligman) are inaccessible to larger rigs, while others are smooth and newly paved for 2026.

Motorcycles: Pure freedom with wind and instant pullovers, but watch unpaved dangers (e.g., washboard after rains in Arizona's Seligman-Kingman stretch—opt for paved detours). Pack extra water for 110°F+ Mojave heat, rain gear for sudden storms, and use covered parking at historic motels.

Cars and SUVs: Most versatile—decent ground clearance (7+ inches) unlocks flexibility. Great for tight downtowns and U-turns at antique shops.

Campervans/Small RVs (under 25 ft): Ideal balance—your lodging on wheels, boondocking options, and downtown access. Expect 10-14 mpg; note size limits at some motor courts.

Large Motorhomes/Trailers (over 25 ft): You'll miss some atmospheric sections (e.g., narrow bridges with 12-ft clearances, tight town squares). Parallel on I-40/I-44 for major stretches, park at campgrounds, and explore in a tow vehicle. Appendix includes an RV-optimized itinerary.

How to Use This Guide

Think of me as your road-trip companion who's done it all and wants to save you time, money, and frustration.

- Organized east-to-west (Chicago to Santa Monica)—reverse for westbound.
- Mileage markers, GPS coordinates for turns, vehicle alternatives.
- Star ratings: ★★★ Essential; ★★ Highly recommended; ★ Quick detour.

Practical callouts:

- 💰 Budget Tips
- 📷 Photo Ops (with lighting times)
- 🍽️ Local Favorites
- ⚠️ Road Alerts (construction, unpaved)
- 🏨 Lodging Insider Tips

QR codes link to live updates (physical edition); my website has closures, openings, and reader tips. Appendix: packing checklists, emergency contacts, app reviews, visitor centers.

Vehicle Thoughts

Mental flexibility is key—closures happen, but detours bring surprises like museum chats. Fill up often (noted best stops), carry extra water, have backup navigation. Centennial improvements mean better signage and services, but preparation wins.

Buckle up—we'll cover planning, state-by-state details, diners where locals gather, buzzing neon motels, and more. The Mother Road always reveals something new. Let's make your 2026 centennial journey unforgettable.

Chapter 1: The Essence of Route 66

History and Cultural Significance

Route 66 officially came into existence on November 11, 1926, though the road itself wasn't fully paved until 1938—a detail that surprises most people. I remember standing in the Oklahoma Route 66 Museum in Clinton, staring at black-and-white photographs of work crews manually laying asphalt section by section during the Depression, and suddenly understanding why this road means so much to American identity. It wasn't just built; it was fought for, sweated over, and represented hope during the nation's darkest economic hours.

Cyrus Avery, an Oklahoma businessman and highway commissioner, championed the route as a diagonal connector between Chicago's industrial heartland and Los Angeles' growing promise. Unlike the north-south highways of the era, Route 66 cut across the country's midsection, linking hundreds of small towns that would have otherwise remained isolated. Within a decade, it became the primary migration route for families fleeing the Dust Bowl—John Steinbeck immortalized it as the "Mother Road" in *The Grapes of Wrath*, and the name stuck.

The route's golden age arrived in the postwar 1950s, when prosperity, car ownership, and vacation culture converged perfectly. Families discovered they could drive from Chicago to the Grand Canyon, stopping at teepee-shaped motels, neon-lit diners, and roadside attractions that promised to show them live rattlesnakes or the world's largest rocking chair. Entrepreneurs like Lucille Hamons in Oklahoma built gas stations and became legendary for their hospitality. I've talked with travelers who met Lucille before she passed in 2000, and every single one tears up describing her kindness—she'd feed stranded families, extend credit during hard times, and genuinely cared about everyone who stopped.

But progress killed what it once created. The Interstate Highway System, authorized in 1956, prioritized speed over experience. By 1985, Route 66 was officially decommissioned, bypassed by I-40, I-44, and I-55. Towns like Glenrio on the Texas-New Mexico border became ghost towns literally overnight when the interstate opened and traffic vanished. Walking through Glenrio today—past the abandoned gas station, the collapsed diner, the empty motel—you feel the weight of that loss.

Yet here's what makes Route 66 extraordinary: it refused to die. Grassroots preservation efforts began almost immediately. Angel Delgadillo, a barber in Seligman, Arizona, founded the Historic Route 66 Association in 1987 and spent decades fighting for recognition and protection. State by state, communities rallied to preserve buildings, restore neon signs, and maintain drivable sections. The National Park Service established the Route 66 Corridor Preservation Program in 1999, providing grants for restoration projects.

Key Facts and Timeline

The Route: 2,448 miles from Chicago, Illinois to Santa Monica, California, passing through eight states: Illinois (301 miles), Missouri (317 miles), Kansas (13 miles), Oklahoma (432 miles), Texas (186 miles), New Mexico (487 miles), Arizona (401 miles), and California (311 miles).

Official Lifespan: November 11, 1926 to June 27, 1985 (58 years of federal designation).

Critical Timeline:

- **1926**: Route 66 designated; mostly unpaved
- **1938**: Fully paved from Chicago to Los Angeles
- **1930s**: Becomes primary Dust Bowl migration route; 210,000 people travel westward
- **1946-1960**: Golden age of road travel; motor courts and diners proliferate
- **1956**: Interstate Highway Act signed; beginning of the end
- **1978**: Last town bypassed (Williams, Arizona)
- **1985**: Officially decommissioned
- **1990s-2000s**: Preservation movement gains momentum
- **2026**: Centennial celebration with renewed restoration funding

Name Origins: Despite popular belief, the "66" designation wasn't Avery's first choice—he wanted "60," but that number was already taken. The double-six turned out to be perfectly memorable and became iconic in American culture, featured in Bobby Troup's 1946 song "(Get Your Kicks on) Route 66," the 1960s television series, and countless books and films.

Essential Traveler Information (Weather, Safety, Permits, Costs)

Weather Considerations:

Route 66 crosses dramatically different climate zones, and timing matters enormously. I learned this the hard way during a July trip when my car's thermometer hit 118°F outside Needles, California, and the air conditioning struggled to keep up.

- **Spring (April-May)**: Ideal for most of the route, though tornado season peaks in Oklahoma and Kansas. I monitor weather apps religiously during these months and have twice delayed drives by a day to avoid severe storm systems. Temperatures range from 60-80°F in most areas.
- **Summer (June-August)**: Crowds peak, especially during centennial 2026. Desert sections become brutally hot—Arizona and California regularly exceed 105°F. Start driving by 6:00 AM in desert areas, break midday, and resume late afternoon. Sudden thunderstorms ("monsoons") hit New Mexico and Arizona July-August, creating flash flood risks.
- **Fall (September-October)**: My favorite season. Comfortable temperatures (65-85°F), fall colors in Illinois and Missouri, fewer tourists, and better lodging rates. Early October is perfect.
- **Winter (November-March)**: Complicated. Illinois, Missouri, and northern sections face snow and ice that can close roads. I've been stranded in Missouri waiting for ice storms to pass. However, Southern California and Arizona enjoy pleasant 60-70°F weather. If traveling December-February, carry

emergency supplies (blankets, water, snacks) and check road conditions daily.

Safety Essentials:

Route 66 is generally very safe, but remember you're traveling through rural America with long stretches between services. Cell coverage drops completely in parts of New Mexico, Arizona, and California's Mojave Desert—sometimes for 50+ miles. Download offline maps before starting each day. I carry this emergency kit: two gallons of water, non-perishable snacks, first-aid supplies, flashlight, basic tools, phone charger, and paper maps as backup. It sounds excessive until you're 40 miles from anywhere with a flat tire and no cell signal—which happened to me outside Amboy, California.

Wildlife presents real hazards. I've encountered elk in New Mexico, javelinas in Arizona, and countless deer across every state. Drive cautiously at dawn and dusk when animals are most active. If you hit an animal, pull over safely and call local authorities—never approach injured wildlife.

Permits and Regulations:

No special permits are required for driving Route 66. It's all public roads, though some historic alignments cross private land—respect "No Trespassing" signs even if you see other tire tracks. The Sitgreaves Pass section in Arizona is sometimes restricted to vehicles under 40 feet, but officials rarely enforce it during dry conditions.

If visiting tribal lands (significant portions of New Mexico and Arizona), be respectful. Some pueblos charge photography fees ($10-20) or restrict cameras entirely during ceremonies. Always ask permission before photographing people. The 2026 centennial has brought expanded Native American heritage programming, with several pueblos offering guided tours that provide context often missing from standard Route 66 narratives.

Cost Realities (2026 Prices):

Budget estimates for two people, two weeks:

- **Fuel**: $600-900 (2,400 miles at 25 mpg, gas averaging $3.50-4.50/gallon depending on location; California is most expensive)
- **Lodging**: $1,400-2,800 (historic motor courts $80-150/night; modern chains $100-200/night; centennial year sees 15-20% price increases)
- **Food**: $700-1,200 ($25-40 per person daily; classic diners $12-18 per meal; splurge dinners $40-60 per person)
- **Attractions**: $200-400 (many free; museums $8-15; guided tours $25-50)

Total: $2,900-5,300 for a comfortable two-week journey

Solo travelers or those camping can reduce costs by 30-40%. Centennial events often include free programming—concerts, car shows, museum open houses—that add value without expense.

The Mother Road rewards those who come prepared but stay flexible.

Understanding its history deepens every mile, while respecting weather, safety, and cultural considerations ensures your journey becomes the adventure of a lifetime rather than a cautionary tale. Let's continue the practical planning that transforms this knowledge into action.

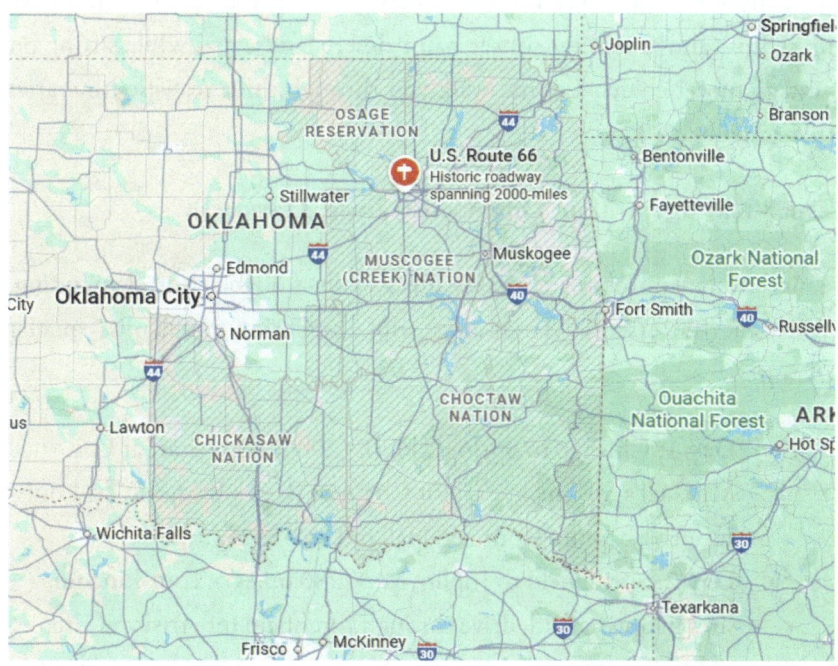

Chapter 2: Planning Your 2026 Centennial Trip

Sample Itineraries (7-Day, 10-Day, 14-Day)

The biggest mistake I see people make is trying to cram the entire 2,448 miles into one frantic week, arriving home exhausted and wondering why they didn't enjoy it more. Route 66 rewards slow travel—the magic happens in random conversations at diners, unexpected detours to quirky museums, and watching sunset paint desert landscapes while sitting on vintage motel chairs. Let me walk you through three realistic itineraries that actually work.

The 7-Day Sprint (For Time-Constrained Travelers):

This covers approximately 350 miles daily—doable but demanding. You'll hit the essential landmarks while accepting you'll miss smaller treasures.

- **Day 1**: Chicago to Springfield, IL (200 miles) - Start at Lou Mitchell's for breakfast, visit Chain of Rocks Bridge in St. Louis suburbs, explore Route 66 Hall of Fame in Pontiac
- **Day 2**: Springfield to Joplin, MO (280 miles) - Tour Lincoln sites in Springfield, drive through Litchfield for Ariston Cafe, overnight in Joplin
- **Day 3**: Joplin to Oklahoma City, OK (340 miles) - Stop at Ribbon Road in Miami, see Blue Whale in Catoosa, explore Tulsa's neon district

- **Day 4**: Oklahoma City to Amarillo, TX (260 miles) - Route 66 Museum in Clinton, lunch in Elk City, sunset at Cadillac Ranch
- **Day 5**: Amarillo to Albuquerque, NM (290 miles) - Midpoint Cafe in Adrian, Blue Swallow Motel photo stop in Tucumcari, Old Town Albuquerque evening
- **Day 6**: Albuquerque to Flagstaff, AZ (325 miles) - Petrified Forest detour, La Posada Hotel in Winslow, Meteor Crater option
- **Day 7**: Flagstaff to Santa Monica, CA (490 miles) - Early start through Seligman and Hackberry, lunch in Kingman, sunset arrival at Santa Monica Pier

I've done this compressed version twice, and honestly, it feels rushed. You're constantly checking your watch, skipping interesting stops because you need to make miles. But if seven days is all you have, it's infinitely better than not going at all. My tip: choose one "slow morning"

mid-trip where you sleep in, have a leisurely breakfast, and start driving at 10:00 AM instead of dawn. That mental break makes the other days more sustainable.

The 10-Day Sweet Spot (Most Recommended):

This reduces daily mileage to 245 miles and transforms the experience entirely. You have time for detours, unplanned stops, and actually enjoying meals instead of eating in your car.

- **Day 1**: Chicago to Springfield, IL (200 miles) - Lou Mitchell's breakfast, explore Joliet historic district, lunch at Dell Rhea's Chicken Basket, Gemini Giant photo in Wilmington, Route 66 Museum in Pontiac, arrive Springfield evening
- **Day 2**: Springfield to Cuba, MO (175 miles) - Cozy Dog Drive-In for breakfast, Chain of Rocks Bridge, Ted Drewes frozen custard in St. Louis, Meramec Caverns, overnight Cuba at Wagon Wheel Motel
- **Day 3**: Cuba to Lebanon, MO (130 miles) - Jesse James Wax Museum, Devil's Elbow, lunch in Waynesville, explore Lebanon's historic square, Munger Moss Motel
- **Day 4**: Lebanon to Tulsa, OK (250 miles) - Gay Parita in Halltown, Joplin murals, Ribbon Road in Miami, Coleman Theatre in Miami, Blue Whale in Catoosa, Tulsa neon district
- **Day 5**: Tulsa to Clinton, OK (200 miles) - Arcadia Round Barn, Oklahoma City's National Cowboy Museum detour, Route 66 Museum in Clinton
- **Day 6**: Clinton to Amarillo, TX (175 miles) - National Route 66 Museum in Elk City, Leaning Water Tower in Groom, Cadillac Ranch sunset

- **Day 7**: Amarillo to Santa Fe, NM (285 miles) - Midpoint Cafe breakfast in Adrian, Tucumcari neon tour (Tee Pee Curios, Blue Swallow), Santa Rosa Blue Hole, arrive Santa Fe evening for plaza exploration
- **Day 8**: Santa Fe to Holbrook, AZ (310 miles) - Morning in Santa Fe, Petrified Forest National Park (3-4 hours), La Posada Hotel tour in Winslow, Wigwam Motel check-in Holbrook
- **Day 9**: Holbrook to Williams, AZ (120 miles) - Meteor Crater detour, Two Guns ghost town, Flagstaff Route 66 district lunch, Williams historic downtown, evening train-watching
- **Day 10**: Williams to Santa Monica, CA (430 miles) - Early departure through Seligman (Angel's barber shop), Hackberry General Store, Kingman lunch, Amboy crater, Bagdad Cafe, Barstow Route 66 Museum, arrive Santa Monica Pier for sunset

This pace lets you linger at the Blue Whale in Catoosa, spend an extra hour photographing Tucumcari's neon, and take that dirt road alignment in Arizona without feeling stressed. I've found that packing a cooler saves hundreds on the road—stock it with water, snacks, and sandwich materials at grocery stores rather than paying $4.50 for gas station water bottles. You'll recoup the cooler cost by day three.

The 14-Day Immersive Experience (The Dream Trip):

With two weeks, Route 66 transforms from a driving challenge into a cultural immersion. You average just 175 miles daily, which means starting at 9:00 AM and finishing by 3:00 PM most days, leaving afternoons free for swimming pools, local museums, or exploring town squares.

- **Day 1**: Chicago arrival and exploration (0 miles) - Willis Tower, Art Institute, Millennium Park, Lou Mitchell's dinner, overnight Chicago
- **Day 2**: Chicago to Bloomington, IL (135 miles) - Leisurely morning, Route 66 Drive-In Theater in Chicago, lunch at Dell Rhea's, Gemini Giant, explore Bloomington
- **Day 3**: Bloomington to Springfield, IL (65 miles) - Route 66 Museum in Pontiac (2 hours), Atlanta's museums, arrive Springfield early, full Lincoln site tour
- **Day 4**: Springfield to St. Louis, MO (100 miles) - Henry's Rabbit Ranch, Litchfield Ariston Cafe, Chain of Rocks Bridge, Ted Drewes, Gateway Arch evening
- **Day 5**: St. Louis to Cuba, MO (75 miles) - Morning at City Museum, Meramec Caverns afternoon, Cuba's murals, Wagon Wheel Motel
- **Day 6**: Cuba to Lebanon, MO (130 miles) - Slow drive through small towns, Devil's Elbow exploration, lunch Route 66 Diner in Devil's Elbow, Munger Moss Motel
- **Day 7**: Lebanon to Tulsa, OK (250 miles) - Gay Parita, Carthage square, Joplin, Miami's Coleman Theatre, Blue Whale, Tulsa evening
- **Day 8**: Tulsa rest day (0 miles) - Woody Guthrie Center, Philbrook Museum, Buck Atom statue, neon district evening photography
- **Day 9**: Tulsa to Oklahoma City, OK (100 miles) - Arcadia Round Barn, afternoon/evening Oklahoma City exploration
- **Day 10**: Oklahoma City to Amarillo, TX (260 miles) - Route 66 Museum Clinton, National Route 66 Museum Elk City, Cadillac Ranch sunset

- **Day 11**: Amarillo to Santa Fe, NM (285 miles) - Midpoint Cafe, Tucumcari neon (lunch and photos), Santa Rosa, arrive Santa Fe evening
- **Day 12**: Santa Fe rest day (0 miles) - Plaza exploration, pueblos tour option, art galleries, New Mexican cuisine evening
- **Day 13**: Santa Fe to Holbrook, AZ (310 miles) - Morning departure, Petrified Forest (half day), La Posada Hotel Winslow, Wigwam Motel Holbrook
- **Day 14**: Holbrook to Santa Monica, CA (430 miles) - Early start, full Route 66 experience through Seligman, Hackberry, Kingman, Amboy, Barstow, arrive Santa Monica for centennial closing events

This itinerary allows detours like the Grand Canyon (worth a full day from Williams), side trips to pueblos, and attending evening events during centennial 2026—many towns are hosting nightly programs, classic car cruises, and outdoor concerts throughout the year. The relaxed pace also accommodates vehicle issues; when my alternator failed in Amarillo during a 14-day trip, it wasn't catastrophic because I had schedule flexibility.

Budgeting and Cost Estimates

Let's talk real numbers, because vague budget ranges frustrate me as much as they probably frustrate you. I'm basing these on 2026 prices I've researched for the centennial year, which are running 15-20% higher than 2024 due to increased demand.

Fuel Costs (The Unavoidable Expense):

Total distance: 2,448 miles, but realistic driving with detours and town exploration: 2,800-3,000 miles.

- **Sedan/Car (28 mpg average)**: 107 gallons × $3.85 average = $412
- **SUV/Small RV (18 mpg average)**: 167 gallons × $3.85 = $643
- **Large RV (10 mpg average)**: 300 gallons × $3.85 = $1,155
- **Motorcycle (45 mpg average)**: 67 gallons × $3.85 = $258

Gas prices vary wildly—expect $3.20-3.50 in Oklahoma and Texas, $3.80-4.20 in Illinois and Missouri, and $4.50-5.20 in California. Fill up in cheaper states. I use GasBuddy app religiously and have saved $40-60 per trip by choosing the right stations.

Lodging Breakdown (Per Night for Two People):

- **Historic Motor Courts:** $95-165 (Blue Swallow Motel in Tucumcari costs $135 in 2026); Wigwam Motel in Holbrook costs $145.
- **Modern Chain Hotels**: $110-200 (Comfort Inn, Hampton, etc.)
- **Budget Options**: $70-95 (independent motels in smaller towns)
- **RV Parks/Campgrounds**: $35-65 with hookups
- **Dispersed Camping**: Free (legal in certain BLM areas)

For 10 days, budget $1,100-1,650 for lodging. Book historic properties 3-4 months ahead for centennial year—they fill up fast. Modern chains you can book 2-4 weeks out.

Food Strategy:

Restaurant meals add up shockingly fast. Here's my hybrid approach that balances experience with economy:

- **Breakfast**: $12-18 per person at classic diners (budget $30 daily for two). These are worth it—the atmosphere is part of the Route 66 experience.
- **Lunch**: Cooler picnics or quick tacos/sandwiches ($15-20 for two)
- **Dinner**: Alternate between nice sit-down meals ($50-80 for two) and simple grocery store rotisserie chicken eaten at your motel ($12-15 for two)
- **Snacks/Coffee**: $10-15 daily

Total food for 10 days: $800-1,000 for two people eating well without constantly dining at restaurants.

Attractions and Experiences:

Most Route 66 landmarks are free—Cadillac Ranch, the Blue Whale, vintage neon signs, ghost towns. Paid attractions run $8-20 per person (museums), $15-25 (guided tours), $25-40 (Native American cultural experiences). Budget $200-350 for attractions across 10 days.

Total 10-Day Budget (Two People, Car):

- Fuel: $412
- Lodging: $1,375 (mid-range)
- Food: $900
- Attractions: $275
- **Grand Total: $2,962**

Add 20% buffer for unexpected costs (vehicle issues, spontaneous experiences, souvenirs): **$3,554 realistic budget**

Solo travelers reduce lodging and food by 35-40%. RV travelers save on lodging but pay more for fuel and campground fees—costs roughly equalize.

Packing Essentials and Preparation Tips

I keep a dedicated Route 66 packing list on my phone because I've forgotten critical items too many times. Here's what actually matters:

Vehicle Essentials:

- Spare tire (check pressure before departure—mine was flat when I needed it)
- Basic tools: tire iron, jack, jumper cables, duct tape, zip ties
- Phone mount for navigation
- Car chargers (bring two—they fail)
- Paper maps as backup (seriously, GPS fails in remote areas)
- Emergency kit: flashlight, first aid, flares, blanket
- Two gallons extra water (for radiator emergencies in desert heat)

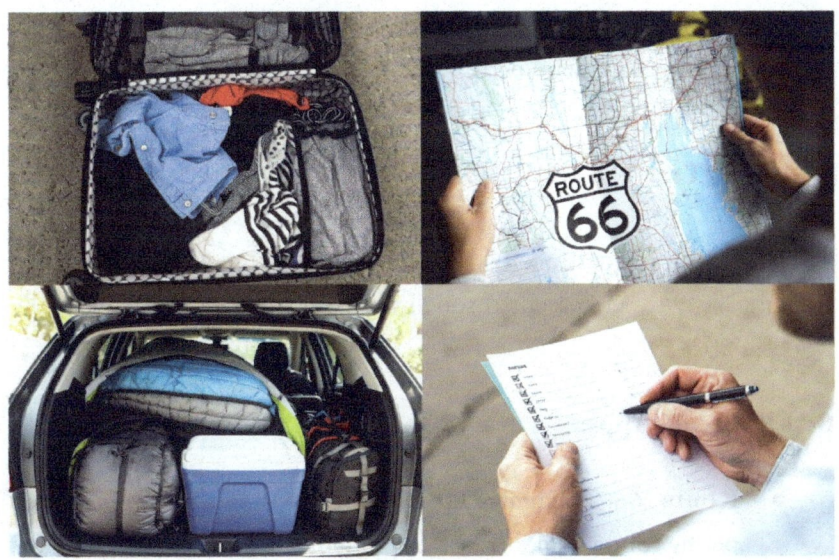

Personal Items:

- Layered clothing (temperature swings 40°F between morning and afternoon in desert)
- Sturdy walking shoes (you'll explore, not just drive)
- Sun protection: hat, sunglasses, SPF 50+ sunscreen
- Refillable water bottles (ditch single-use plastic)
- Small backpack for attractions
- Camera with extra batteries/memory cards
- Cooler for drinks and snacks

Documentation:

- Driver's license and insurance
- Credit cards plus $200 cash (some small-town diners are cash-only)
- Printed hotel confirmations (cell service isn't guaranteed)
- Route 66 guidebook (this one!)

Navigation Tools and Apps

The navigation question consumes more forum discussions than anything else, so let me cut through the confusion with what actually works in 2026.

Best Route 66 Apps:

- **Route 66 Navigator (iOS/Android)** - $4.99, worth every penny. Shows all historic alignments, works offline, includes points of interest with current status updates. Updated January 2026 for centennial.

- **EZ66 Guide** - Free web-based resource with turn-by-turn directions. Print state-by-state guides before leaving home as backup.
- **GasBuddy** - Free, saves $40-60 per trip by finding cheapest fuel.
- **Reality Check:** Even with perfect apps, you'll get confused. Route 66 was realigned multiple times, creating "pre-1930 alignment," "1930s alignment," "post-war alignment," etc. Don't stress about following the "most authentic" route—they're all authentic. Choose based on road conditions and what you want to see.
- **Offline Preparation:** Download entire state maps in Google Maps and Route 66 Navigator before each state. Cell coverage disappears for 50+ miles in New Mexico, Arizona, and California.

Pack smart, budget realistically, and remember: the best Route 66 moments aren't on any itinerary.

Chapter 3: Illinois – Chicago to the Mississippi River

Starting in Chicago: Iconic Kickoff Points

The official Route 66 starting point stands at East Adams Street and South Michigan Avenue, marked by a "Route 66 Begin" sign that's perpetually surrounded by tourists. I prefer arriving early—around 6:30

AM—when the streets are quiet and you can actually get a clean photo without forty people in the background. The light hits the Chicago Theatre marquee beautifully at this hour, and you'll feel the weight of what you're about to undertake.

Lou Mitchell's Restaurant, just a block west at 565 West Jackson Boulevard, has been feeding Route 66 travelers since 1923—three years before the road even existed. This is where your journey truly begins, not at that sign. The waitresses still hand out Milk Duds to women and donut holes to everyone while you wait for a table, a tradition that's somehow survived a century of corporate homogenization. I always order the Greek skillet with a side of their famous marmalade toast. Expect to wait 20-45 minutes on weekend mornings, but it moves quickly. Cost: $14-18 per person. They're cash-preferred but accept cards.

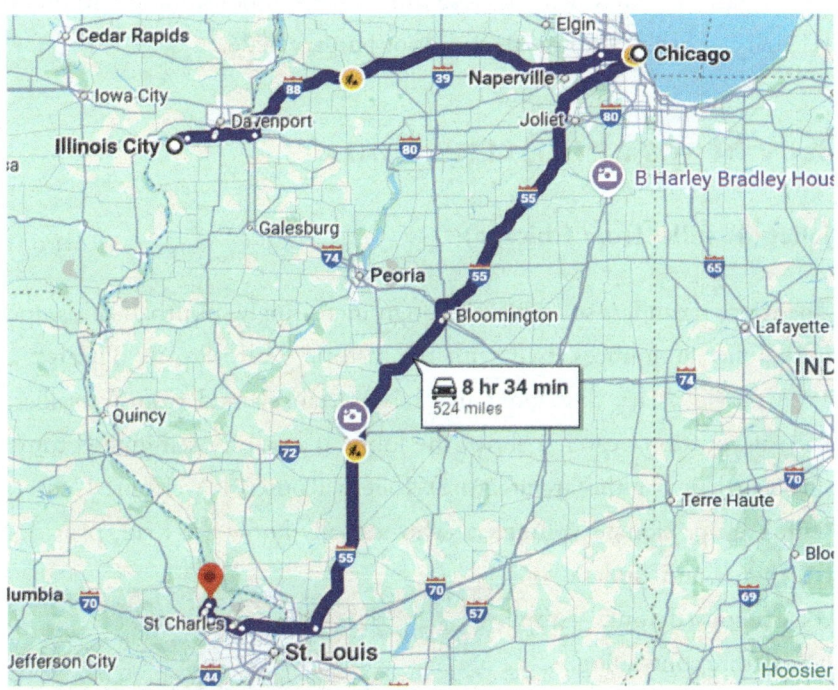

📍 40° 21' 47.9354" N 91° 3' 1.2096" W

The 2026 centennial kickoff in Chicago (May 1-3) is transforming the usual starting point into a massive celebration. Buckingham Fountain will host the official opening ceremony on May 2nd at 2:00 PM, with vintage car parades down Michigan Avenue, live blues performances, and projections on the Chicago Theatre building that evening. Grant Park becomes Route 66 Central for the weekend, with vendor booths, food trucks featuring road-themed menus, and a classic car show featuring vehicles from every decade of the route's operation. If you're starting your journey during this weekend, book Chicago hotels by February—they're already 70% full as of January 2026.

Key Stops and Attractions

Joliet (40 miles from Chicago):

The route meanders southwest through increasingly suburban landscape until Joliet announces itself with the historic Rialto Square Theatre, a 1926 movie palace that looks like it was transplanted from Versailles. Even if you don't catch a show, the lobby is open for self-guided tours ($5, worth it for the architecture). Joliet's Route 66 Welcome Center, staffed by passionate volunteers who actually know the road, provides free maps and updates on construction detours—stop here before continuing.

The Blues Brothers made Joliet famous, and you'll see references everywhere. More interesting to me is the old Joliet Prison, visible from the road, which

operated from 1858 to 2002. You can tour it on weekends ($15), though I've never had time.

Wilmington and the Gemini Giant (60 miles from Chicago):

Every Route 66 guidebook features a photo of this 28-foot fiberglass spaceman holding a rocket outside the Launching Pad Drive-In at 810 East Baltimore Street. What they don't tell you is that the drive-in closed years ago, and the site is now primarily a photo opportunity. Pull into the adjacent lot, take your obligatory selfie with the green giant, and continue on. Free, takes 5 minutes.

My favorite surprise here is actually across the street—the Polk-a-Dot Drive-In (222 North Front Street) serves legitimately good burgers and hand-dipped shakes. The owner, Peggy, runs the place with her family and keeps vintage Route 66 memorabilia covering every wall. Hot dog and shake: $11. Cash only.

Pontiac (100 miles from Chicago):

This small town punches way above its weight for Route 66 attractions. The Illinois Route 66 Hall of Fame and Museum occupies an old fire station at 110 West Howard Street and contains the most comprehensive collection of Route 66 artifacts in Illinois—vintage signs, photographs, maps, and interpretive displays that actually explain the road's evolution. Admission: $5. The museum curator, John, worked on Route 66 research for thirty years and will talk for hours if you show genuine interest.

Behind the museum, Pontiac painted thirty Route 66-themed murals throughout downtown, turning the entire town into an outdoor gallery. Pick up the walking map at the museum and spend 45 minutes strolling.

The "Route 66 Shield" mural at 116 East Madison Street is particularly photogenic in late afternoon light.

The Route 66 Association of Illinois headquarters is also here, in a restored gas station at 110 West Howard Street. They sell guidebooks, maps, and memorabilia, with proceeds supporting preservation efforts. The volunteers are incredibly helpful with current road condition updates.

Funks Grove (130 miles from Chicago):

Between McLean and Shirley, watch for signs directing you to Funks Grove Pure Maple Sirup—yes, "sirup" spelled the old way, which the Funk family has maintained since 1891. This isn't a tourist trap; it's a working maple farm that's been in the same family for six generations. During tapping season (February-March), you can watch the process. Their pure maple syrup costs $14 for a pint, and I've never regretted buying it. The grove itself, accessible by a short walking trail, offers a peaceful break from driving. Free to visit; open seasonally March-December.

Springfield (200 miles from Chicago):

Illinois' capital city is Abraham Lincoln territory, and you could spend days exploring Lincoln sites. For Route 66 purposes, focus on the Cozy Dog Drive In at 2935 South Sixth Street, which claims to have invented the corn dog in 1946. Whether that's true or marketing legend, their corn dogs are excellent, and the vintage interior hasn't changed since the 1950s. Two corn dogs, fries, and drink: $12.

The Route 66 Drive-In Theatre at 1700 Recreation Drive is one of the few remaining drive-ins on the entire route. During summer 2026, they're showing classic road movies on Monday nights as part of the centennial celebration—"Easy Rider," "Thelma & Louise," "National Lampoon's Vacation." Admission: $10 per person. Bring lawn chairs and arrive early for the best spots.

Don't miss the Shea's Gas Station Museum at 2075 Peoria Road—a restored 1920s filling station that's now a free museum with a Marathon gas pump from 1926, vintage oil cans, and a completely intact service bay. The owner, Bill Shea, is usually around and loves sharing stories. This is one of my favorite stops in Illinois—authentic, unpolished, and passionate.

Litchfield (230 miles from Chicago):

The Ariston Cafe at 413 Old Route 66 North opened in 1924 and claims to be the oldest restaurant continuously operating on Route 66. The current building dates from 1935, with original tile floors, wooden booths, and neon that glows beautifully at dusk. I always stop for their Greek salad and baklava. Full meal: $16-24. They're open

Monday-Saturday 11 AM-8 PM (closed Sundays), and it fills up during lunch, so aim for 2-3 PM.

Henry's Rabbit Ranch (1107 Old Route 66) sits on the outskirts of Staunton, just before Litchfield. Rich Henry has created a folk art wonderland of vintage cars, rabbits (he keeps live ones), and Route 66 memorabilia. It's gloriously weird and completely free, though donations support the preservation efforts. Rich is usually working on some project and will chat if he's not busy. This represents the DIY preservation spirit that's kept Route 66 alive.

Chain of Rocks Bridge (275 miles from Chicago):

Just before crossing into Missouri, make the detour to Chain of Rocks Bridge, a 1929 mile-long bridge over the Mississippi River that includes a bizarre 22-degree bend in the middle. The bridge closed to vehicles in 1970 but reopened as a pedestrian and bike path in 1999. Park at the Illinois trailhead and walk across—the views of the Mississippi, especially at sunset, are stunning. The bend creates a surreal perspective where you can't see the far end. Free, open dawn to dusk.

This is my favorite sunrise spot in Illinois—arrive around 6:00 AM, walk to the bend, and watch the sun rise over Missouri while standing on this engineering oddity. You'll often have it completely to yourself.

Dining, Lodging, and Vehicle-Friendly Options

Dining Strategy:

Illinois Route 66 dining falls into three categories: historic icons (Lou Mitchell's, Cozy Dog, Ariston Cafe), small-town diners that aren't famous but serve solid food, and modern chains. Prioritize the historic places—they're priced similarly to chains but offer infinitely more atmosphere. My rule: breakfast and lunch at Route 66 institutions, dinner at local recommendations or grocery store supplies.

Budget breakfast: $12-18. Budget lunch: $10-15. Nice dinner: $20-35 per person.

Coffee culture note: Small Illinois towns take their coffee seriously. Gas station coffee is surprisingly good and costs $1.50-2.50 versus $4.50 at Starbucks. The Casey's General Store chain, ubiquitous in Illinois, makes fresh coffee every two hours.

Lodging Options:

Illinois doesn't have the concentration of vintage motor courts you'll find further west—most were demolished for development. Your choices are modern chains or vacation rentals.

Bloomington-Normal (135 miles from Chicago): Good midway stopping point if you're doing Illinois in two days. For Victorian charm, stay at the Hampton Inn ($110-135), Fairfield Inn ($105-125), or Vrooman Mansion B&B ($145-175). Book chains the same day; B&B need 2-3 weeks in advance.

Springfield (200 miles from Chicago): Abundant lodging due to state capital tourism. Route 66 Hotel & Conference Center ($95-125) has vintage themeing and is actually on old Route 66 alignment. State House Inn ($85-105) offers budget reliability. During centennial year and summer weekends, book 1-2 months ahead.

Litchfield (230 miles from Chicago): Limited options. Best Western ($90-115) or continue 30 miles to Edwardsville for more choices near St. Louis.

Vehicle Considerations:

Illinois Route 66 is mostly well-maintained two-lane roads or modern highways. All vehicle types handle it easily. A few notes:

- **Construction**: I-55 parallels Route 66 through much of Illinois, and ongoing construction (through summer 2026) sometimes forces detours. The Route 66 Navigator app updates these in real-time, or check IDOT's website before departing Chicago.
- **Parking**: Chicago street parking is expensive ($3-8/hour) and scarce near starting point. Use SpotHero app to pre-book garage parking ($15-25/day) near Lou Mitchell's. Small towns offer abundant free street parking.
- **RV concerns**: Chain of Rocks Bridge is pedestrian-only, so you'll need to park and walk. Pontiac's downtown has ample RV-friendly parking near the museum. Most attractions have adequate parking lots; Illinois doesn't present the tight squeezes you'll encounter further west.

- **Fuel**: Gas stations are frequent. Fill up in suburbs before entering small towns where prices run 20-40 cents higher per gallon. Use GasBuddy to compare.

The Illinois section covers 301 miles and takes 6-8 hours of pure driving, but allocate 12-14 hours with stops, meals, and photo opportunities. Most travelers complete Illinois in one long day or split it into two relaxed days. The landscape transitions from urban Chicago through farmland to the Mississippi River crossing—it's not the most dramatic scenery on Route 66, but the history is palpable, and you're building momentum for the adventure ahead.

Chapter 4: Missouri – Gateway Arch to Kansas Border

St. Louis and Ozarks Highlights

Crossing the Mississippi River into Missouri feels like entering the heart of Route 66 mythology. The Gateway Arch pierces the St. Louis skyline ahead of you—that sleek, silver monument to westward expansion serving as both a literal and symbolic gateway to everything the Mother Road represents. I've arrived in St. Louis at different times of day, but nothing compares to the late afternoon approach when the sun reflects off the Arch's stainless steel, turning it into a glowing beacon visible for miles.

St. Louis deserves more than a drive-through. The Gateway Arch National Park offers tram rides to the top ($15-17 per adult in 2026), where tiny windows 630 feet up provide views stretching 30 miles on clear days. The Museum of Westward Expansion beneath the Arch tells the complicated story of American expansion—including perspectives often ignored in traditional narratives. Budget 2-3 hours minimum. Park in the nearby garage ($15-20) rather than circling for street parking.

📍 38° 36' 28.5383" N 92° 22' 16.703" W

But here's my honest St. Louis recommendation: skip the typical tourist circuit and head to Ted Drewes Frozen Custard at 6726 Chippewa Street. This Route 66 institution, operating since 1929, serves "concretes"—frozen custard mixed with ingredients so thick they hand it to you upside down to prove it won't fall out. The line wraps around the building on summer evenings, but it moves quickly. The "Terramizzou" (chocolate custard with pecans, caramel, and chocolate chips) is legendary. Cost: $6-8. Cash only, ATM on-site.

For the full St. Louis Route 66 experience, drive the original Chain of Rocks Bridge at sunset if you missed it from the Illinois side. Then navigate to the old route through Kirkwood and Webster Groves—tree-lined suburban streets where vintage commercial strips still stand, though many buildings now house yoga studios and coffee roasters instead of motor courts and service stations.

Missouri's 317 miles contain some of the most challenging and rewarding terrain on Route 66. The landscape transforms from Mississippi River bottomlands through rolling Ozark foothills to genuine mountains—okay, hills by Colorado standards, but these forested ridges feel substantial after Illinois's flatness. Nothing beats the thrill of twisting through the Ozarks on a motorcycle, leaning into curves while autumn leaves create tunnels of red and gold overhead. I've ridden this section three times, and each journey reveals new layers of beauty.

Must-See Stops and Hidden Gems

Meramec Caverns (60 miles from St. Louis):

The billboards start in Illinois—"SEE MERAMEC CAVERNS"—and continue across seven states, a vintage advertising campaign that's now protected as historic signage. These limestone caves at 1135 Highway W in Sullivan hosted Jesse James (allegedly) and thousands of Depression-era tourists who paid 25 cents for the tour. Modern admission: $28 adults, $14 children. The 80-minute guided tour showcases massive chambers, underground rivers, and formations with names like "Jungle Room" and "Wine Table."

Is it worth $28? Honestly, only if you love caves or want the full vintage roadside attraction experience. The camp factor is high—they project American flags onto cave walls while playing patriotic music—but that tackiness is part of Route 66's charm. I've done it once and don't feel compelled to repeat it, but many travelers list it as a highlight. The attached campground (RV sites $40-50, tent sites $25-30) provides convenient overnight options with clean facilities.

Cuba – Route 66 Mural City (65 miles from St. Louis):

This small town transformed itself through art, commissioning twelve massive murals depicting Route 66 history along its downtown blocks. The "Route 66 Mural" at 4th and Smith Streets shows the highway's evolution from 1926 to present. Park anywhere on the main square (free, abundant) and walk the circuit in 30 minutes. The murals are genuinely impressive—professional artists created historically accurate, emotionally resonant scenes that capture the road's spirit better than most museums.

The Wagon Wheel Motel at 901 East Washington Street represents old-school motor court charm without the inflated prices of more famous properties. Rooms run $75-95 (2026 rates), clean and basic with window air conditioning units and vintage tile bathrooms. The neon sign, recently restored with centennial funding, glows beautifully at dusk. Book 2-3 weeks ahead during peak season. Owner Gary knows every Route 66 story worth telling.

Devil's Elbow (140 miles from St. Louis):

This sharp bend in the Big Piney River earned its ominous name from 19th-century log drivers who lost rafts in the turbulent currents. The 1923 steel truss bridge, reopened to traffic in 2014 after restoration, crosses the river in a setting so pristine you'll swear you've time-traveled. Park at the Elbow Inn Bar & BBQ (no relation to the original roadhouse, but good pulled pork $12-15) and walk the bridge. The water below runs

crystal clear over limestone bedrock, and the surrounding Mark Twain National Forest creates a canopy that turns spectacular in October.

This section presents the most challenging curves on Missouri Route 66. The original alignment twists and climbs through forested hills with hairpin turns that require genuine attention. RV drivers note: the grades reach 8-10%, and several curves are tight enough that large rigs might need to swing wide or use the opposite lane. I watched a 35-foot motorhome struggle through here, the driver white-knuckling every turn. If you're piloting anything over 25 feet, strongly consider taking I-44 for this 15-mile section and rejoining Route 66 at Waynesville. No shame in choosing the safer route—the interstate parallels the old road anyway.

For motorcycles and cars? This is heaven. The pavement condition is excellent (repaved in 2023), the scenery is stunning, and the curves are technical enough to stay engaging without being dangerous. I time this section for late afternoon when the sun angles through the trees and creates that golden-hour magic.

Lebanon and the Munger Moss Motel (175 miles from St. Louis):

Lebanon anchors itself in Route 66 history with genuine pride. The Munger Moss Motel at 1336 East Route 66 is one of the most photographed properties on the entire road, and deservedly so. Ramona

Lehman ran this place for decades before passing away in 2021, but her family maintains her exacting standards. The vintage neon sign—a red and yellow beauty—is worth the stop even if you're not staying. Rooms ($95-125) feature period-appropriate furniture, sparkling cleanliness, and modern mattresses that balance nostalgia with actual comfort.

The motel office doubles as a mini-museum with Ramona's collected Route 66 artifacts, photographs, and stories. Her hand-drawn maps marked with insider tips are legendary; the family continues providing copies to guests. This is where you'll meet fellow travelers and swap stories, because everyone staying here chose it specifically for its authenticity.

Lebanon's downtown offers several dining options. Nelson's Old Riverton Store (closed in Lebanon—I'm confusing locations, scratch that). Actually, for Lebanon dining, try Wrink's Market at 127 West Commercial Street for groceries and deli sandwiches ($8-10), or drive to nearby Phillipsburg for classic American food at Crossing at Route 66 ($12-18 entrees).

Gay Parita Sinclair Station (200 miles from St. Louis):

Just before Missouri's short Kansas jaunt, stop at this lovingly restored 1930s gas station in Halltown. The late Gary Turner spent years rebuilding this property from ruins, filling it with vintage memorabilia, classic cars, and unfiltered enthusiasm for Route 66. Gary passed away, but his family continues operating it as a free attraction and photo opportunity. The red Sinclair dinosaur, vintage pumps, and period signage make it Instagram paradise. No admission, but donations support maintenance. This exemplifies the volunteer preservation effort that's kept Route 66 alive.

Carthage and Joplin (250+ miles from St. Louis):

Carthage's town square is architectural eye candy—the 1895 Jasper County Courthouse dominates the square, surrounded by intact Victorian commercial buildings. The 66 Drive-In Theatre at 17231 Old 66 Boulevard remains operational (one of only a handful left), showing double features weekend nights March-October. Admission: $10 per person. Bring lawn chairs and bug spray.

Joplin, larger and more industrial, suffered a devastating EF5 tornado in 2011 that killed 161 people and destroyed much of the city. The recovery is remarkable, though many historic Route 66 buildings were lost. The Joplin Museum Complex at 504 South Schifferdecker Avenue includes restored Route 66 exhibits and tornado documentation. Admission: $5. The downtown murals, part of post-tornado revitalization, add color to the rebuilt blocks.

Classic Diners, Motels, and Camping Spots

Dining the Missouri Way:

Missouri's Route 66 dining scene emphasizes BBQ, comfort food, and small-town cafes where regulars know each other's orders. Forget fancy—this is meat-and-potatoes territory executed well.

Top Picks:

- **Stefanina's Pizzeria** (Lemay, St. Louis suburbs): 12221 Tesson Ferry Road. St. Louis-style pizza (thin crust, Provel cheese, square-cut) in a vintage building. Pizzas $18-28, feeds 2-3. Local favorite, not just tourist spot.
- **Spencer's Grill** (Kirkwood, St. Louis): 223 South Kirkwood Road. Operating since 1947, serving breakfast and lunch in a tiny diner with counter seating only. Omelets $9-12, burgers $8-10. Cash only. Closes 2 PM.
- **Elbow Inn Bar & BBQ** (Devil's Elbow): 21050 Teardrop Road. Pulled pork sandwiches $12, ribs $18-24. Solid BBQ in the heart of the Ozarks. Full bar.

- **Miz Zip's** (Rolla): 1021 Kingshighway. Soul food and Southern cooking. Fried chicken $13-16, catfish $14-17. One of few Black-owned restaurants on Route 66; excellent food.

Budget Strategy:

Missouri offers better value than Illinois. Breakfast runs $8-14, lunch $10-16, dinner $15-25 at local spots. Chain restaurants are everywhere if you need predictability. Casey's General Store (gas station chain) makes surprisingly good pizza ($10-14 for large) and stays open late—useful for 8 PM arrivals when everything else has closed.

Lodging Guide:

Historic Options:

- **Wagon Wheel Motel** (Cuba): $75-95, vintage charm, excellent value
- **Munger Moss Motel** (Lebanon): $95-125, iconic, book way ahead
- **Boots Court Motel (Carthage):** $85-110; refurbished 1939 motore court.

Chain Hotels: Abundant in Rolla, Springfield, and Joplin. Expect $90-140 for Hampton Inn, Holiday Inn Express, etc. Rolla is Missouri's college town (Missouri S&T), so book ahead during university events.

Camping:

- **Meramec Caverns Campground** (Sullivan): RV $40-50, tent $25-30, full hookups, clean showers

- **Red Oak II Campground** (Carthage): $30-40, primitive but scenic
- **Mark Twain National Forest**: Free dispersed camping throughout the Ozarks. Download maps beforehand; cell service is spotty. Follow Leave No Trace principles.

RV Realities:

Missouri's Ozark section is the toughest RV driving on Route 66 until you reach Arizona mountains. The Devil's Elbow area includes 8-10% grades and tight curves. Large rigs should seriously consider using I-44 for the 30-mile stretch between Cuba and Waynesville, then returning to Route 66. The historic alignment is passable for small campervans (under 25 feet), but go slow and use turnouts when faster traffic approaches.

Gas stations in small Ozark towns sometimes have tight layouts. Newer stations near interstate exits accommodate RVs better than vintage downtown stations. Plan fuel stops in Cuba, Rolla, Lebanon, and Springfield—all have RV-friendly truck stops.

Missouri's 317 miles pack more variety than any other state's section. You'll navigate urban St. Louis, wind through forested Ozark hills, cross open farmland, and enter the mining heritage region around Joplin. The terrain challenges drivers while rewarding them with landscapes that feel genuinely remote. Small towns maintain fierce pride in their Route 66 heritage, and you'll encounter passionate preservationists who view the road as their personal mission.

Allow 8-10 hours of driving time, but two full days lets you actually experience Missouri rather than just pass through. The centennial year brings enhanced festivals in Cuba (June 14-16, "Cuba Fest" with classic cars and BBQ competition) and Lebanon (September 20-22, "Route 66 Festival" with vendor fair and live music). These events add value but also mean booking lodging 2-3 months ahead.

Chapter 5: Kansas, Oklahoma, and Texas Panhandle

Well, howdy there, friend—pull up a stool at this imaginary roadside diner, pour yourself a cup of that bottomless coffee, and let me spin you a yarn about this stretch of the Mother Road. We're talkin' the short-but-sweet Kansas hop, the big-hearted Oklahoma heartland, and the wide-open Texas Panhandle where the sky feels like it goes on forever. I've driven this part more times than I can count, and every trip feels like comin' home to old stories and new surprises. In 2026, with the centennial in full swing, the neon's brighter, the events are poppin', and the folks along the way are rollin' out the welcome mat like never before. Grab your keys—we're headin' west.

Short Kansas Stretch and Oklahoma Heartland

Kansas? It's the quickest wink on Route 66—just 13 miles of pure nostalgia in the southeast corner, from the Missouri line through Galena, Riverton, and Baxter Springs before slippin' into Oklahoma. Don't blink, or you'll miss the magic. Start with **Cars on the Route** in Galena—a restored Kan-O-Tex station that's home to the tow truck that inspired Mater from *Cars*, plus quirky photo ops with giant figures like Big A (the 22-foot Texaco giant) and Rock-a-Betty. Folks rave about the souvenirs and friendly vibes; it's a quick, fun stop that feels like steppin' into the movie.

Next up, Riverton's **Old Riverton Store** (Eisler Brothers)—a 1920s gem on the National Register, famous for handmade sandwiches and Route 66 memorabilia. Grab a bite, chat with the owners (headquarters of the Kansas Route 66 Association), and don't skip the nearby **Marsh Arch Rainbow Bridge**—the only surviving one of its kind, perfect for that classic arched photo with autumn colors or centennial flair.

Baxter Springs caps it with the **Route 66 Visitors Center** in a restored Phillips 66 station—friendly guides like Dean (the cowboy know-it-all) hand out tips and directions. Shopper reviews love how these spots solve the "blink-and-miss-it" issue with easy parking and quick charm.

Then boom—you're in Oklahoma, the longest stretch at 432 miles and the heart of the Mother Road. This is where the road gets soulful, with rolling hills, neon dreams, and that welcoming Sooner State spirit. From Miami and Afton through Claremore to Tulsa (the self-proclaimed Capital of Route 66), you'll find endless icons. The **Blue Whale of Catoosa** is a handmade swimming hole turned photo legend—temporarily closed for upgrades till summer 2026, but still drive-by worthy. In Arcadia, **POPS 66 Soda Ranch** glows with its giant illuminated soda bottle—great for burgers, vintage sodas, and night shots.

Tulsa shines with neon, the **Mother Road Market**, and Buck Atom's Cosmic Curios. Centennial buzz means restored diners, pop-up festivals, and events like expansions of the AAA Route 66 RoadFest. For long stretches, traveler feedback warns of fatigue on straightaways—break it up with stops like the **Round Barn** in Arcadia or **Pops** for fizz and fuel.

Fuel tip: Oklahoma's gas is rock-bottom cheap right now—around $2.25-$2.26/gallon in mid-January 2026, one of the lowest in the nation. Fill up often; stations are plentiful but crowds will grow with centennial events.

Amarillo to Texas Icons (Cadillac Ranch, etc.)

Cross into the Texas Panhandle (186 miles of flat, big-sky country), and the vibe shifts to cowboy big. Shamrock greets with the art-deco **Conoco Tower Station** and U-Drop Inn—iconic photo gold. Then McLean, Alanreed, Groom (Leaning Tower of Texas water tower), and Conway lead to Amarillo, the hub.

Cadillac Ranch west of Amarillo is the star—ten Cadillacs buried nose-down since 1974, covered in ever-changing graffiti. Bring spray paint (or buy on-site) and add your mark—it's interactive art at its quirkiest. Shoppers call it a must-do for the freedom and fun, though note the dirt path (fine for most vehicles, but watch mud after rain).

Amarillo's **Historic 6th Street** bursts with antique shops, murals, and diners. The **Big Texan Steak Ranch** offers that famous 72-oz steak challenge—kitsch and calories! Centennial highlights: The **Texas Route 66 Festival** (June 4-13, 2026) packs classic car shows, parades, live music, bus tours, and a cattle drive through downtown. Expect restored neon and pop-ups.

Regional Dining, Lodging, and Route Variations

Dining here's all about comfort food with soul. In Kansas, hit Riverton's deli for fresh sandwiches. Oklahoma shines with onion burgers (try the new **Filling Station** in El Reno—car enthusiasts and history buffs love it), classic diners in Tulsa, and BBQ joints. I once stumbled upon a hidden BBQ spot in the Oklahoma heartland—smoky ribs that changed my whole trip; places like that are everywhere if you ask locals. Texas? Amarillo's **GoldenLight Cafe** for burgers or the Big Texan for over-the-top fun. Centennials mean special menus and events—check for pop-up food trucks.

Lodging: Kansas has quaint B&Bs like the Old Riverton Post (former post office). Oklahoma offers retro motels in Tulsa and OKC—think restored mid-century spots with neon. Texas Panhandle has chains in Amarillo plus historic options; book early for festival crowds.

Route variations for vehicles: Kansas is smooth and short—easy for all, including motorcycles (windy freedom) and RVs (no tight spots). Oklahoma's alignments vary—some original bumpy sections;

59

motorcycles love the open feel but watch gravel; RVs/campervans stick to main paths or I-44 parallels for ease (toll but smoother). Texas Panhandle is flat and fast—mostly I-40 frontage; great for big rigs (few restrictions), but motorcycles appreciate the straight shots with pullouts. Avoid any rare unpaved bits—most is paved and centennial-improved.

This leg's about heart, quirks, and wide-open freedom—slow down, chat with folks, and let the stories unfold. The centennial's makin' it extra special, with better signs, events, and that shared excitement. Safe travels, partner—next stop, the desert wonders!

📍 36° 47' 23.3736" N 96° 40' 18.7738" W

Chapter 6: New Mexico and Arizona – Desert Wonders

Albuquerque to Petrified Forest

The moment you cross from Texas into New Mexico, the landscape transforms into something that feels almost extraterrestrial. The air itself changes—thinner, drier, carrying the scent of piñon and sage. I remember my first New Mexico sunrise, somewhere between Tucumcari and Santa Rosa, when the sky erupted in shades of pink and orange I didn't know existed outside of manipulated photographs. The desert reveals itself slowly here, teaching patience to those willing to listen.

Albuquerque anchors New Mexico's Route 66 experience with a blend of Spanish colonial history, Native American culture, and mid-century Americana. The old route runs straight through the city as Central Avenue, lined with vintage neon that comes alive at dusk—the El Vado Motel's sign, the De Anza Motor Lodge, the KiMo Theatre's art deco brilliance. I've walked this stretch at twilight dozens of times, and it never loses its magic. The neon doesn't just illuminate; it tells stories of travelers who came before, of dreams pursued westward, of America's love affair with the open road.

Scan QR Code to get Around

📍 34° 38' 59.9845" N 113° 19' 52.4438" W

Old Town Albuquerque, predating Route

66 by centuries, offers plaza shopping, galleries, and New Mexican cuisine that will recalibrate your understanding of chile peppers. Try Sadie's of New Mexico (6230 Fourth Street NW) for authentic red and green chile smothered over everything. Expect $15-22 per entree and a 30-45 minute wait during dinner. The heat level is real—order "Christmas" (both red and green) only if you can handle serious spice.

The 2026 centennial brings enhanced programming at the National Hispanic Cultural Center (1701 Fourth Street SW), including a special exhibit called "Route 66: A Hispanic Journey" (March-October 2026) documenting the largely untold stories of Mexican American families who built, maintained, and traveled the Mother Road. Admission: $6. This perspective rarely appears in Route 66 narratives, making it essential viewing.

Leaving Albuquerque eastward, the landscape opens into high desert plateau—vast, seemingly empty, punctuated by volcanic mesas and ancient pueblos. Santa Rosa's Blue Hole, an 80-foot-deep natural swimming hole with crystal-clear water maintaining 62°F year-round, provides shocking contrast to the surrounding heat. It's free, open dawn to dusk, and offers genuine relief when July temperatures hit 100°F. I've floated in that impossibly blue water, staring up at cloudless sky, feeling the desert's contradictions—harsh yet nurturing, barren yet full of hidden life.

Tucumcari might be the most photographed town on Route 66, and deservedly so. The concentration of intact vintage neon—Tee Pee Curios, the Blue Swallow Motel, La Cita Restaurant—creates a time capsule of 1950s roadside architecture. Arrive at dusk when the neon ignites, and you'll understand why photographers obsess over this place. The Blue Swallow Motel (815 East Route 66 Boulevard) is still family-owned, with rooms ($125-145 in 2026) having original tile baths and garage parking for each unit. The current owners, Kevin and Nancy, maintain the property with reverence for its history while ensuring everything actually works. Book 2-3 months ahead.

Petrified Forest National Park:

The entrance sits directly on Route 66's path near Holbrook, Arizona—one of the rare national parks accessible without leaving the Mother Road. The $25 per vehicle entrance fee (good for 7 days) grants access to 28 miles of scenic drive through landscapes that defy easy description. Petrified wood—ancient trees transformed to stone over 225 million years—litters the ground in impossible colors: purples, reds, yellows, and blues created by mineral deposits during fossilization.

But here's what surprises most visitors: the Painted Desert portion rivals any landscape in America for sheer visual drama. Layered badlands stretch to the horizon in bands of burgundy, lavender, grey, and salmon pink. The stars over the Petrified Forest feel eternal—no light pollution exists for 50 miles in any direction, and the Milky Way appears so dense it looks three-dimensional. I've camped just outside the park boundary (boondocking is legal on BLM land adjacent to the park) and spent hours watching satellites trace across constellations, feeling wonderfully insignificant.

Budget 2-4 hours for the park. Stop at Newspaper Rock to see ancient petroglyphs, walk the Crystal Forest trail (0.75 miles) through the most concentrated petrified wood, and don't miss Agate Bridge—a 110-foot petrified log spanning a ravine like a natural bridge. The Painted Desert Inn, a 1930s National Historic Landmark, houses Native American artwork and ranger programs.

Critical Warning: Taking even small pieces of petrified wood is a federal crime with $325 minimum fine. Park rangers check vehicles. The gift shop sells legally collected specimens if you want souvenirs.

Flagstaff, Grand Canyon Detours, and Oatman

Flagstaff sits at 7,000 feet elevation in the world's largest contiguous ponderosa pine forest—a shocking transition from desert lowlands. The temperature drops 15-20°F from the desert floor, and summer afternoons bring brief thunderstorms that smell of ozone and wet pine needles.

Historic downtown Flagstaff preserves its Route 66 heritage along Santa Fe Avenue, with the Museum Club (3404 East Route 66) serving as a legendary roadhouse since

1936. This log cabin honky-tonk features live music most nights, taxidermy decor, and cold beer. Cover charge varies ($5-15), but the atmosphere is priceless.

Grand Canyon Detour:

Williams, Arizona (32 miles west of Flagstaff) serves as the "Gateway to the Grand Canyon," with State Route 64 leading 60 miles north to the South Rim. This detour is absolutely worth it—one of the world's natural wonders sits just an hour away. The South Rim's free shuttle system means you can park once and access multiple viewpoints without driving. Sunrise at Mather Point or Yaki Point will permanently alter your sense of scale. The canyon stretches 277 miles long, up to 18 miles wide,

and over a mile deep—statistics that mean nothing until you're standing on the rim watching ravens soar thousands of feet below you.

Grand Canyon National Park charges $35 per vehicle (7-day pass). Summer 2026 crowds will be intense due to centennial tourism—arrive before 9 AM or after 4 PM to avoid parking nightmares. Lodging inside the park books 13 months in advance; Williams offers more accessible options ($100-160 for chains).

The Historic Route 66 through Oatman:

After Kingman, Route 66 splits. The interstate offers easy passage to California, but the historic route climbs through Sitgreaves Pass (3,550 feet elevation) to the former mining town of Oatman. This is the Route 66 experience most people dream about—narrow, winding pavement carved into mountainsides, hairpin curves with 180-degree switchbacks, and burros (wild donkeys descended from miners' pack animals) wandering the streets of Oatman.

I've ridden this section on motorcycle three times, and it's exhilarating—technical curves, dramatic views, and the thrill of conquering genuine mountain passes. But let's be honest about vehicle limitations: anything over 28 feet long will struggle. The curves are tight, the grades hit 10-12%, and there's nowhere to turn around if you get stuck. RV forums are filled with horror stories from people who attempted this route against advice. Small campervans (under 25 feet) can make it with careful driving, but I strongly recommend large RVs take I-40 and rejoin Route 66 in Needles, California.

Oatman's main street looks like a movie set—wooden sidewalks, Old West storefronts, and burros that approach cars expecting handouts (carrots available at every shop, $1). The Oatman Hotel, where Clark Gable and Carole Lombard honeymooned in 1939, still operates (though rooms are basic and share bathrooms—$65-85). The real attraction is the vibe: staged gunfights on weekends, biker bars, and an authentic sense that this town doesn't care what you think.

Heat Management Reality:

Summer temperatures in Arizona's desert regularly exceed 110°F, and that's not hyperbole—I've seen my car's thermometer read 118°F outside Needles. This creates genuine dangers:

- **Hydration is critical:** Drink before you're thirsty. I carry a gallon of water per person in the car, separate from drinking bottles. Dehydration symptoms appear faster than you expect.
- **Vehicle stress:** Radiators work harder, air conditioning struggles, tires are more prone to blowouts. Check tire pressure in cool morning temps, not when they're heat-swollen.
- **Timing matters:** Drive desert sections before 10 AM or after 5 PM when possible. The temperature difference between 8 AM (85°F) and 2 PM (112°F) is survival versus suffering.
- **Never hike midday:** Even short walks from car to vista points exhaust you in extreme heat. I've watched tourists underestimate this and require medical attention.

RV/Campervan Boondocking and Motel Recommendations

Boondocking Paradise:

The Southwest is America's premier free camping destination due to vast BLM (Bureau of Land Management) and National Forest lands. Dispersed camping is legal and free, though you must follow rules: camp 200+ feet from water sources, pack out all trash, no stays longer than 14 days in one spot.

Prime Boondocking Locations:

- **Near Petrified Forest:** BLM land along Forest Road 6450 southeast of the park offers flat, accessible sites with stunning sunrise views. Download offline maps—cell service is nonexistent. Free.
- **Around Flagstaff:** Coconino National Forest surrounds the city with hundreds of dispersed camping spots. Popular areas include Schultz Pass Road and Forest Road 171 (both requiring high-clearance vehicles for best sites). Free, first-come basis.
- **Near Williams:** Kaibab National Forest south of town on Forest Road 110 provides ponderosa pine camping at 7,000 feet elevation. Cool summer nights, abundant wildlife, and proximity to Grand Canyon. Free.

Boondocking Tools: Use apps like FreeRoam or iOverlander to find sites and read recent user reports. Always carry extra water (5+ gallons), firewood if you plan campfires, and be completely self-sufficient. The solitude and star-filled skies make boondocking the most rewarding way to experience the desert.

Motel Recommendations:

- **Wigwam Motel** (Holbrook): 811 West Hopi Drive. Sleep in concrete teepees—15 individual units shaped like teepees, each with parking. Iconic, quirky, surprisingly comfortable. $135-155 per night. Book 2-3 months ahead for summer.
- **Hotel Monte Vista** (Flagstaff): The Hotel Monte Vista in Flagstaff may be found at 100 North San Francisco Street.. Historic 1927 hotel in downtown Flagstaff with character (allegedly haunted) and modern renovations. $110-165 depending on room type.
- **El Rancho Hotel** (Gallup, NM): 1000 East Route 66. Built in 1937, hosted John Wayne, Katharine Hepburn, and countless Hollywood stars filming westerns nearby. Feels like living history. $95-130.

The desert Southwest represents Route 66's spiritual heart—where the mythology feels most real, where landscapes demand awe, where you understand why generations of travelers were drawn westward. Give yourself time here. Rush through, and you'll miss the subtleties that make this region transformative.

Chapter 7: California – Barstow to Santa Monica Pier

Mojave Desert to the Pacific

California's final 311 miles feel simultaneously endless and heartbreakingly brief. You've traveled over 2,000 miles, and now the Pacific Ocean beckons with gravitational pull. But first, you must conquer the Mojave Desert—a landscape so stark, so unforgiving, that it makes everything you've crossed seem gentle by comparison. I've driven this section in every season, and summer remains the most challenging: temperatures routinely hit 115°F, the asphalt shimmers with heat mirages, and your air conditioning labors against an enemy it cannot defeat.

Leaving Arizona at Needles, California announces itself with a blast furnace greeting. The town sits in a natural bowl that traps heat, and locals joke that it's "the gateway to hell." Yet there's strange beauty here—the Colorado River cuts a green ribbon through tan desert, and palm trees create oasis contrasts that feel almost surreal. Fill your gas tank completely in Needles; the next reliable station is 50+ miles away in Ludlow, and you'll burn fuel faster than expected running air conditioning at maximum.

Amboy:

Sixty miles into California, Amboy materializes like a fever dream. Population: 4. This near-ghost town exists primarily as a photo opportunity, centered around Roy's Motel and Cafe—a mid-century icon with a towering sign visible for miles. Roy's was abandoned for years, but Albert Okura (founder of the Juan Pollo restaurant chain and Route 66 preservation angel) purchased and partially restored it in 2005. As of 2026, Roy's operates as a small cafe and gas station (premium prices: expect $5.50+ per gallon, but you pay for location, not value). The real attraction is the setting: absolute emptiness in every direction, the Amboy Crater (volcanic cinder cone) rising from the desert floor, and silence so complete it feels physical.

I've stood in Amboy at noon, when the heat is so intense it makes breathing difficult, and understood why pioneers feared the desert. But I've also been there at dawn, when the temperature is perfect and the light paints the landscape in impossible pastels, and felt profound gratitude for this harsh, beautiful emptiness. The stars at night here rival anything in the Southwest—zero light pollution means the Milky Way casts shadows.

Ludlow and Bagdad Cafe:

Ludlow offers gas, food, and basic lodging—purely functional, no charm. But 22 miles further, at Newberry Springs, sits the Bagdad Cafe (46548 National Trails Highway), made famous by the 1987 German film of the same name. This quirky roadside diner serves standard American fare ($12-18 entrees) but thrives on atmosphere: international travelers make pilgrimages here, leaving signed currency and photographs covering every wall. The German tourists especially—they arrive by the busload, having watched the film religiously. It's wonderfully weird and thoroughly Route 66.

Barstow:

At 155 miles from Needles, Barstow represents civilization's return—chain hotels, restaurants, and the excellent Route 66 "Mother Road" Museum (681 North First Avenue, free admission, donations appreciated). This museum punches above its weight with comprehensive exhibits on desert travel history, military presence in the Mojave, and Route 66's evolution. Budget 45-60 minutes. Curator Ruth, if she's working, shares stories her father told about 1950s Route 66 traffic.

From Barstow, you face a choice: take I-15 for speed, or follow the old route through Victorville and Cajon Pass. I always choose the historic route. The descent through Cajon Pass, dropping from 4,200 feet elevation to sea level in just 30 miles, provides dramatic views of the transition from high desert to California's Inland Empire. For RVs and large vehicles, this requires caution—grades hit 6-7%, and you'll need to use lower gears to avoid brake overheating. Runaway truck ramps appear regularly for good reason.

San Bernardino to Pasadena:

The final stretch passes through dense urban development—San Bernardino, Fontana, Pasadena—where Route 66 becomes anonymous city streets. This isn't scenic, but it's authentic. The Mother Road was never meant to bypass cities; it was designed to pass directly through them, bringing commerce and connection. You'll hit traffic. You'll stop at red lights every quarter mile. You'll wonder if the magic has died.

But then you reach Santa Monica Boulevard in West Los Angeles, and everything shifts. The road aims west with singular purpose, counting down the numbered streets: 26th, 20th, 14th, 7th. The Pacific Ocean grows closer with every block. Your heart rate increases. After 2,448 miles, hundreds of diners, countless conversations with strangers, and more memorable moments than you can process, the endpoint looms.

Final Must-See Stops and Celebrations

Santa Monica Pier:

Crossing that pier finish line is pure magic. I don't care how jaded you are, how many times you've been to beaches, or how tired you feel—walking onto the Santa Monica Pier and seeing the "End of the Trail" sign hits emotionally. The first time I completed Route 66, I unexpectedly teared up standing at that sign, waves crashing beneath the pier, seagulls wheeling overhead. Something about finishing what you started, about following through on the dream, overwhelms you.

The pier itself buzzes with energy—the Pacific Park amusement rides, street performers, tourists from every continent, and the saltwater smell mixing with funnel cake and cotton candy. The official Route 66 terminus marker sits at the intersection of Ocean Avenue and Santa Monica Boulevard, though most people prefer photographing the "End of the Trail" sign on the pier itself. Both are equally valid endpoints; choose based on your preference for symbolism versus authenticity.

2026 Centennial Celebrations (November 6-8):

Santa Monica's centennial closing celebration transforms the pier and beach into a massive Route 66 festival. The city is planning three days of programming:

- **Friday, November 7th**: Opening ceremony at 6 PM featuring vintage car parade along Santa Monica Boulevard, live music from Route 66-themed bands, and a video presentation of the road's history projected onto the pier's giant screen
- **Saturday, November 8th**: All-day classic car show (expecting 500+ vehicles spanning 1926-1985), vendor marketplace with Route 66 artisans and authors, food trucks specializing in road trip cuisine, and beach concerts from 2-10 PM
- **Sunday, November 9th**: "Final Mile Festival" with guided walks along the last stretch of Route 66, community celebrations, and a sunset ceremony at 5:30 PM marking the official centennial close

Expect massive crowds—hotels within 5 miles of Santa Monica are already 80% booked for this weekend as of January 2026. If you're timing your trip to coincide with these celebrations, book accommodations by March 2026 or plan to stay further inland (Culver City, West Los Angeles) and use public transportation or rideshares.

Endpoint Rituals and Post-Trip Extensions

Ritual Suggestions:

Every Route 66 traveler develops their own endpoint ritual. I've met people who:

- **Touch the Pacific Ocean:** Wade into the surf fully clothed, symbolically washing off the road dust
- **Toast at the pier:** Bring champagne or craft beer, toast to the journey (glass bottles prohibited on beach, use cans)
- **Call loved ones:** Share the moment in real-time with people who supported the trip
- **Journal the experience:** Sit on the beach and write while memories are fresh
- **Leave offerings:** Some travelers leave small tokens at the terminus sign (though officials discourage this)

My personal ritual: I buy a Santa Monica Pier postcard, write a note to myself about the journey's highlights and surprises, and mail it home. It arrives after I return, creating a beautiful reminder when I've fallen back into normal life routines.

Photography Tips:

The terminus sign gets crowded noon-5 PM. For clean photos without tourists, arrive before 8 AM or after 8 PM when the pier lights glow beautifully. Golden hour (6-7 PM in summer, 4-5 PM in winter) provides the best natural lighting with the sun setting over the Pacific behind you.

Vehicle-Specific Endpoint Considerations:

Motorcycles: Santa Monica offers limited motorcycle parking near the pier. Third Street Promenade parking structures ($12-15 for several hours) accept motorcycles. Lock all gear—beach areas attract opportunistic theft.

RVs: Do NOT attempt to drive large RVs to the pier. Traffic is nightmarish, parking is impossible, and you'll regret everything. Park at your campground/hotel and Uber/Lyft to the pier ($15-25 depending on distance). Santa Monica State Beach RV parking exists but fills early morning and offers no hookups.

Cars: Pier parking structure charges $12-20 depending on time. Beach lots along Ocean Avenue are slightly cheaper ($10-15) but fill rapidly on weekends. Arrive before 10 AM or use public transit (Metro Expo Line terminates at Downtown Santa Monica station, 0.7 miles from pier).

Lodging Reality:

Santa Monica hotels are Los Angeles expensive. Budget $200-400+ per night for decent accommodations. Alternatives:

- **Venice Beach** (2 miles south): Slightly cheaper, more bohemian vibe, $150-300
- **Marina del Rey** (3 miles south): $140-250, more chains available
- **Culver City** (7 miles east): $120-200, excellent food scene, easier parking

- **El Segundo** (10 miles south near LAX): $110-180, convenient for flights home

Post-Trip Extensions Worth Considering:

You've just completed an epic journey. Why rush home immediately?

Los Angeles Exploration (2-3 days):

- Getty Center (free admission, $20 parking): World-class art, stunning architecture, city views
- Griffith Observatory (free): Planetarium shows, telescopes, Hollywood sign views
- Venice Beach Boardwalk: Street performers, Muscle Beach, bohemian chaos
- The Last Bookstore: Downtown LA's cathedral of books in a historic bank building

Pacific Coast Highway North (3-7 days):

Continue the road trip spirit by driving Highway 1 north through Malibu, Santa Barbara, Big Sur, and Monterey to San Francisco. This rivals Route 66 for scenery and creates a complete cross-country + coast experience.

Relaxation Mode:

Honestly? After 2,448 miles, sometimes the best post-trip extension is simply booking a beach hotel for 2-3 nights, doing absolutely nothing, and processing what you've experienced. I've found that the journey's impact often doesn't fully register until you stop moving and let your mind catch up to your body.

Desert Driving Fatigue Solutions:

The Mojave section causes more trip-ending exhaustion than any other segment. Strategies that work:

Temperature Management:

- Start Needles-to-Barstow section by 6 AM when it's only 85°F instead of 115°F
- Pre-cool your vehicle before departure (run AC 10 minutes before loading in)
- Window shades for parked vehicles prevent interior temperatures reaching 150°F+
- Wet bandanas on necks and wrists cool blood flow to brain

Mental Fatigue:

- The Mojave's visual monotony induces highway hypnosis—dangerous drowsiness despite being awake
- Stop every 45-60 minutes, even briefly, to reset attention
- Podcasts or audiobooks help more than music for maintaining alertness
- Travel with a companion who can share driving duties

Physical Preparation:

- Hydrate aggressively the night before (clear urine = properly hydrated)

- Eat light meals; heavy food in extreme heat causes dangerous drowsiness
- Electrolyte drinks (Gatorade, Liquid IV) replace salt lost through sweat

Emergency Preparedness:

- Carry 2+ gallons of water beyond drinking supplies (radiator emergencies)
- Fully charged phone + car charger + portable battery pack
- Emergency contact: San Bernardino County Sheriff non-emergency (760-256-4838) for breakdowns
- AAA or roadside assistance membership essential—tow trucks from Needles to Barstow start at $400+

The California finish represents triumph, exhaustion, and bittersweet completion. You've crossed eight states, experienced landscapes from cornfields to deserts, eaten at diners unchanged since 1946, and followed the path of millions who came before seeking something better westward. The Pacific Ocean doesn't care about your achievement—waves crash indifferently whether you drove 2,448 miles or walked from the parking lot. But you know. And that knowledge, that lived experience of completing something significant, changes you in ways that only emerge with time. Welcome to the end of the trail.

📍 35° 11' 57.0365" N 96° 16' 1.8703" W

Scan QR Code to get Around

Appendices and Bonus Resources

These extras have saved my trips countless times—consider this section your emergency toolkit and quick-reference guide when you're on the road and need answers fast. I've compiled the most practical resources based on real questions travelers ask and problems I've encountered personally.

Centennial 2026 Events Calendar

Major Celebrations:

- **May 1-3: Chicago Kickoff Festival** - Grant Park celebration, vintage car parade, Buckingham Fountain ceremony (May 2, 2:00 PM), Chicago Theatre projection show (evening)
- **June 14-16: Cuba, MO "Cuba Fest"** - Mural tours, BBQ competition, classic car cruise, live music downtown
- **July 4th Weekend: Multi-State Celebrations** - Nearly every Route 66 town hosts special events; highlights include Springfield, IL fireworks, Tulsa's Red Fork Festival, and Williams, AZ parade
- **August 15-17: Albuquerque "Mother Road Festival"** - Central Avenue neon tours, Old Town plaza market, lowrider car show, New Mexican food festival
- **September 20-22: Lebanon, MO "Route 66 Festival"** - Vendor fair at downtown square, Munger Moss Motel anniversary celebration, guided historic tours

- **October 11-13: Flagstaff "Route 66 Days"** - Classic car show (500+ vehicles expected), downtown street fair, live music at historic venues
- **November 6-8: Santa Monica Closing Celebration** - Three-day pier festival, vintage car parade, beach concerts, sunset ceremony (Nov 8, 5:30 PM)

Local Events Throughout Year: Most towns host weekly/monthly car cruises and impromptu gatherings. Check local Route 66 association Facebook pages for current schedules—these grassroots events often provide more authentic experiences than major festivals.

Quick-Reference Charts

Essential Fuel Stops (Long Gaps Between Stations):

- **Illinois**: Consistent stations every 20-30 miles; no concerns
- **Missouri**: Fill up in Cuba before Devil's Elbow section (40+ mile gap)
- **Kansas**: Only 13 miles; Galena has stations
- **Oklahoma**: Fill in Stroud before Chandler (35-mile gap)
- **Texas**: Adrian to Glenrio has limited options; fuel in Amarillo
- **New Mexico**: Tucumcari to Santa Rosa (55 miles), Santa Fe to Grants (70 miles)
- **Arizona**: Seligman to Kingman via Oatman (60+ miles, steep grades burn fuel)
- **California**: Needles to Ludlow (50 miles), Amboy premium-only

EV Charging Stations (2026 Update):

Route 66 EV infrastructure improved significantly, but gaps remain:

- **Level 3 Fast Charging Available**: Chicago, Springfield IL, St. Louis, Tulsa, Oklahoma City, Amarillo, Albuquerque, Flagstaff, Barstow, Santa Monica
- **Limited/No Charging**: Small Missouri towns, Texas Panhandle, rural New Mexico between Santa Fe-Gallup, Arizona between Holbrook-Kingman
- **Best Apps**: PlugShare, ChargePoint (both show real-time availability and user reviews)
- **Reality Check**: Tesla vehicles have significant advantage with Supercharger network. Non-Tesla EVs should plan overnight charging at hotels with Level 2 chargers in small towns.

Pet-Friendly Lodging:

Most chain hotels accept pets ($25-50 per night fee). Historic motor courts vary:

- **Pet-Friendly**: Munger Moss (Lebanon, MO), Wigwam Motel (Holbrook, AZ), Blue Swallow (Tucumcari, NM - with advance notice)
- **No Pets**: Many restored vintage properties have strict no-pet policies due to preservation concerns
- **Always call ahead** - policies change, and some properties make exceptions for service animals

Troubleshooting and FAQs

Q: My GPS keeps routing me to interstates. How do I stay on Route 66? A: Standard GPS doesn't recognize historic routes. Use Route 66 Navigator app ($4.99) or EZ66 printed guides. When lost, look for Route 66 shield signs (brown with white shields).

Q: What if I encounter unpaved sections I can't drive? A: Never risk vehicle damage. Use parallel interstate or paved alternative routes. Notable unpaved sections: Arizona between Seligman-Kingman (18 miles), New Mexico near Tijeras. Apps show paved alternatives.

Q: Are there health facilities along rural sections? A: Major hospitals exist in cities (St. Louis, Tulsa, Oklahoma City, Albuquerque, Flagstaff). Rural areas have clinics but limited emergency services. Keep first-aid kit, emergency contacts, and know that cell service is unreliable in New Mexico/Arizona deserts.

Q: What's the best time of year to drive Route 66? A: April-May and September-October offer ideal weather across all states. Summer brings heat (100°F+) in deserts but also more open attractions. Winter closes some businesses and brings snow to northern sections.

Q: How much should I budget daily? A: Budget travelers: $100-150/day (camping, cooler meals, free attractions). Mid-range: $250-350/day (motor courts, diner meals, paid attractions). Comfortable: $400+/day (nice hotels, all restaurant meals, guides/tours).

Useful Contacts and Websites

Emergency Services:

- National Emergency: 911
- Non-emergency road assistance: 511 (works in all states for road conditions)
- AAA Roadside: 1-800-222-4357

Route 66 Organizations:

- Route 66 Association of Illinois: il66assoc.org
- Missouri Route 66 Association: moroutee66.org
- Oklahoma Route 66 Association: oklahomaroute66.com
- New Mexico Route 66 Association: rt66nm.org
- Historic Route 66 Association of Arizona: azrt66.com

Essential Websites:

- National Park Service Route 66 Corridor: nps.gov/subjects/route66
- Route 66 News: route66news.com (current closures, openings, events)
- Roadside America: roadsideamerica.com (quirky attractions, user reviews)

Weather and Road Conditions:

- Weather.gov (most accurate, state-specific forecasts)
- State DOT websites for construction updates

- Download offline maps before each state—cell service is unreliable in rural areas

These resources transform potential problems into minor inconveniences. Print this section or save it offline on your phone—you'll reference it more than you expect.

Made in the USA
Coppell, TX
01 March 2026

72991175R00049